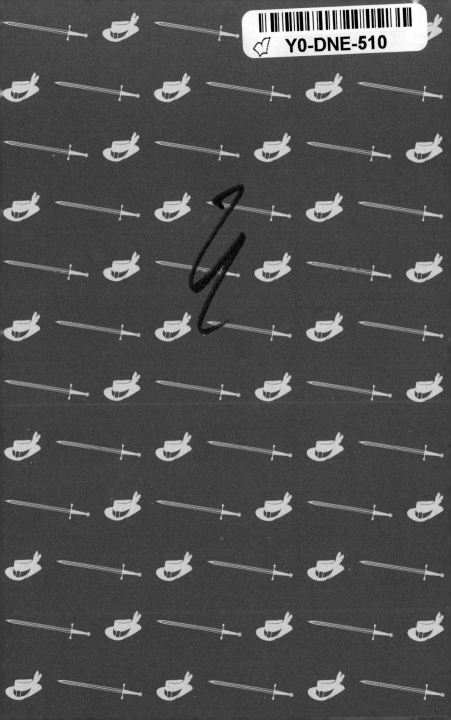

The THREE MUSKETEERS

hinkler

hinkler

Published by Hinkler Books Pty Ltd
45–55 Fairchild Street
Heatherton Victoria 3202 Australia
www.hinkler.com

© Hinkler Books Pty Ltd 2010, 2020

Abridged adaptation written by Archie Oliver
Original story written by Alexandre Dumas
Cover illustration: Laura Stitzel
Illustrations by Terry Riley, Szilvia Szakall, and Nadene Naude

ISBN: 978 1 4889 2050 9

First Printing: June 2020

Printed and bound in Guangdong, China

The THREE MUSKETEERS

ALEXANDRE DUMAS

The Author

Alexandre Dumas (1802–1870)

The French novelist and dramatist Alexandre Dumas was a popular nineteenth century writer of historical fiction. He was the son of a general in the French army.

He produced many books in his lifetime, but *The Three Musketeers* and *The Count of Monte Cristo* were his most famous. Both were translated into many different languages and were later adapted into feature films, television series, and cartoon productions.

Dumas wrote two sequels to *The Three Musketeers* —*Twenty Years After* and *The Viscount of Bragelone*. Neither of the sequels was as successful as the first book in the trilogy.

His literary career also included works on such subjects as art, travel, crime, and cookery. In his lifetime, he produced more than 250 books, plays, and other literary works.

Dumas' son, also known as Alexandre, became a writer too.

Contents

A Guide to Some of the Key Characters

Young **D'Artagnan,** his faithful old horse **Methuselah,** and his bold right-hand man, **Planchet**.

The serious musketeer **Athos** and his manservant, **Grimaud**.

The larger-than-life musketeer **Porthos** and his manservant, **Mousqueton**.

The wise musketeer **Aramis** and his manservant, **Bazin**.

Captain Treville: Captain of the King's Musketeers.

Cardinal de Richelieu: the power behind the throne of France. His spies and agents include the beautiful and mysterious **Milady,** the arrogant **Count de Rochefort,** and **Madame Lannoy**. The Cardinal's band of ace swordsmen include **Jussac, Bernajoux, Bicarat,** and **Cahusac**.

King Louis XIII: the King of France; a man who fears both the Cardinal's power and the political and romantic intrigues of **Anne,** his Spanish Queen.

The Duke of Buckingham: the Englishman who loves the Queen of France.

Lord de Winter: an English gentleman who knows Milady's true identity.

Mademoiselle Bonacieux: the Queen's lady-in-waiting and D'Artagnan's first love.

Monsieur Bonacieux: Mademoiselle Bonacieux's treacherous uncle.

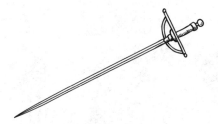

Chapter 1

D'Artagnan and a Horse Named Methuselah

Early one morning in 1626, a humble, handsome, and hot-tempered young Frenchman named D'Artagnan rode into the harbor town of Calais, in France. His ancient horse, Methuselah, trotted obediently through the busy streets.

The youngster was just eighteen years old, but already the strongest man in his home village. He was on his way to Paris, to seek fame and fortune

with the King of France's illustrious Musketeers.

But something happened in Calais that day—
an event that set D'Artagnan on a dangerous path;
a fearful road bloodied by murder, mystery, and
intrigue. The incident led to him being involved in
a war between France and England, with English
duke and French count at each other's throats, and
spies from both nations on each other's trails.

It also left the young D'Artagnan in love with
one woman, for whom he would risk all.

There was another woman who would come
into his life too; a murderous vixen of a creature
who would come to hate D'Artagnan more than
any other man. Only his death would let her rest.

And all this, which was to come in the future,
happened just because a man insulted
D'Artagnan's old horse!

***

On that fateful morning, D'Artagnan rode into
the yard of the Jolly Miller's Inn, to water his
horse.

Methuselah was indeed an ancient old nag. He

had lost every single hair from his tail. His coat had faded to a pale straw color, and his ears hung tattered and torn. But D'Artagnan loved that horse. It had loyally carried him for most of his young life.

So he wasn't very happy when an arrogant gentleman descended from a coach outside the inn and roared with laughter when he saw Methuselah.

"Send that horse to the butcher's," guffawed the man. "He's only fit to be turned into horse meat now!"

D'Artagnan was blinded by fury. He walked across to the gentleman, his old bent sword dangling from his belt. As he neared the man, he remembered the words of farewell that his father had given him, as he had left home the day before.

"Remember you are a gentleman," he'd said. "Your ancestors go back many hundreds of years. Take no insult from anyone, except our King Louis. Never fear a quarrel, and avenge every insult."

"Pray sir," said D'Artagnan. "What are you

laughing at?"

"It could be the horse," replied the man, with a smirk.

"If you laugh at my horse, sir," cried D'Artagnan, "would you dare laugh at its rider?"

"If I felt like it," the man answered, with a swagger. "I shall laugh at who and what I please."

D'Artagnan drew out his sword. "And will you laugh at my horse now? Apologize to my horse or I'll strike you!"

"I never apologize, least of all to a horse," said the man, without a hint of humor.

"Turn and fight!" demanded D'Artagnan.

The man continued to walk away, and D'Artagnan stepped forward and pricked him on the backside with his sword.

The gentleman, tall and well built, turned around. His cruel black and piercing eyes were now blazing with fury. "Young man," he said, "you clearly have no idea who I am, but you shall suffer for your cheek."

"And you, sir," replied D'Artagnan, rather too

boldly, "may not know that I am about to join Captain Treville and the King's Musketeers."

"Dropping such big names won't save you," said the man, drawing his sword and attacking the young man.

D'Artagnan leaped forward to meet him, spotting a vivid red scar from an old sword wound on the man's cheek as he did so. Their swords clashed and battle commenced.

And what a sword fight it was!

The good people of Calais awoke that morning to the sounds of the battle outside the Jolly Miller's Inn. Some wondered if it was King Louis' Musketeers battling Cardinal Richelieu's Guards. Others imagined England had invaded France. And some reckoned it was just local scoundrels making war on everyone else.

But, when they looked out of their windows, the townspeople saw neither the colors of the King's Musketeers, those braggarts and devil-may-care fighters, nor the red and yellow standard of Cardinal Richelieu's men. And all the local rogues were still abed.

They were astonished to see that the noise came from just two men.

The man with the scar was as good a swordsman as D'Artagnan had ever met, but nobody scared the young man. He parried, cut, and slashed with great skill. And after ducking and diving for nearly half an hour, D'Artagnan struck the man a fierce blow, piercing him in the thigh.

The man let out a scream of pain. He backed off, staring at D'Artagnan with a murderous look on his face. D'Artagnan was not to know that his opponent was one of the most dreaded and cruel men in France.

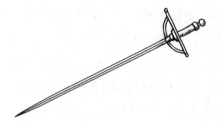

Chapter 2

Milady

"Apologize," said D'Artagnan, watching the man take a few steps back, "or I'll have another piece of you."

The man sneered at D'Artagnan and waved his arm toward three of his armed menservants, who were standing nearby watching the fight.

"Get rid of this bothersome young fly!" he shouted, before walking away to his carriage. "I can't be fighting with young fools like him."

"Coward!" cried D'Artagnan, chasing him and catching him another final blow before his rescuers arrived.

The three men, armed with swords and truncheons, attacked young D'Artagnan.

Now outnumbered, D'Artagnan fought on bravely but without any real hope. The three men knocked him down and he hit his head on the ground.

As he drifted in and out of consciousness, D'Artagnan became aware of the smell of a woman's perfume. It had a very particular scent. He peered up through half-closed eyes and saw a beautiful young woman. She was twenty-five years old at most, and had deep blue eyes, and blond hair that tumbled down over her shoulders.

"Tie him on his horse and send him packing," ordered the woman, who was clearly used to being obeyed. "Let him go back to his nursemaid."

"The devil I will!" cried D'Artagnan, recovering his wits and struggling to his feet again.

He was about to chase the three men who had

attacked him. But the woman tripped him up and kicked him violently in the stomach.

"Behave, fool!" she screamed, her eyes glaring with a madness that shocked D'Artagnan. "Finish him off, men!"

D'Artagnan lifted his sword and lunged at the three men again. But, at last, the enemy got the better of him and laid him unconscious on the ground once more—this time breaking his sword in two, to add insult to injury.

***

When he awoke, D'Artagnan found he was lying on a bed in the inn. His possessions, held in a single bag, were still with him. But when he looked through the bag he found that one item was missing.

It was a letter from his father to Captain Treville, the commanding officer of the King's Musketeers. D'Artagnan's father and Treville were old friends. They'd fought for the King in recent wars. The letter contained a request to give his son all help in joining the Musketeers.

D'Artagnan was furious at finding the letter had been stolen. He was pretty sure it must have been the man with the scar.

Just then, he heard voices beneath his window. He stumbled over, every bone in his body aching, and looked out. It was the same man and he was talking to the lady who had attacked him. Once more he noticed the smell of her expensive perfume, rising up to his window.

"The Cardinal has ordered you to return to England, Milady," the gentleman was saying. "You're to keep watch on the Duke of Buckingham. Follow his every movement. If he comes to France again, don't let him out of your sight for a second. And if he goes near the King's palace, kill him!"

D'Artagnan was intrigued at how the man called her *Milady* all the time. It was almost as if he daren't speak her name.

The woman started to walk away, but suddenly looked up and saw D'Artagnan.

She smiled at him icily. "Running home to your nursemaid today?" she asked.

That was too much for D'Artagnan. He leaped from his window, drawing his broken sword in mid-air.

This time it was the woman who signaled to three of her servants standing by her coach. "Get that wretch out of my sight!" she yelled.

Once more D'Artagnan was attacked and overpowered. The woman came up and gave him one last painful kick. "If we meet again," she said with a chilling matter-of-factness, "I shall kill you."

The man and the woman boarded their separate carriages and went their different ways, he to Paris and she to England.

That evening, D'Artagnan set out on the same road to Paris, riding his ancient horse and clutching his broken sword. He traveled south, little knowing that he had not only met the most dangerous man in France, but also the country's most murderous woman.

And it wasn't to be the last time that D'Artagnan met the wicked couple.

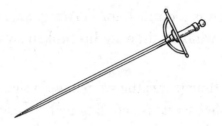

Chapter 3

Arrival in Paris

When he reached Paris, D'Artagnan found his way to the barracks of the King's Musketeers. They stood close to the Louvre, the grand palace of King Louis of France.

D'Artagnan was directed to a small fortress, the headquarters of Captain Treville. He was ushered into the captain's office where a man whom he took to be Captain Treville was lecturing three musketeers.

"Athos! Porthos! Aramis! You'll be the death of me," the man was saying. "Cardinal Richelieu has reported to me that you have been attacking his guards again. Six of his men, killed!"

"Captain Treville," said one of the three, "we were attacked first."

"We were not looking for a fight, sir," said the second.

"We were bound to defend the King's name," said the third.

D'Artagnan's father had told him all about the rivalry between the King's Musketeers and Cardinal Richelieu's Guards. The Cardinal was the King's chief minister and had the right to have his own private army.

But the musketeers were the King's bodyguards, and jealously guarded their role. The musketeers liked nothing better than to find an excuse to fight the Cardinal's men—to the death if honor demanded it.

"You know that the King supports your attacks where he can," continued Treville. "But he can't be seen to favor you over the Cardinal's men. You must not attack his men . . . well, not unless you're sure no one is watching. Now, my young lads; be gone and try to behave yourselves."

Captain Treville, as D'Artagnan found out later, loved his men as if they were his sons.

The three men left and Treville saw D'Artagnan waiting. "Now what can I do for you, young man?" he asked.

"My name is D'Artagnan and I have come to learn to be a musketeer," said D'Artagnan nervously. "You knew my father. I did have a letter for you from him, but it was stolen from me."

"I knew your father well," replied Treville, "and I will gladly help his son. But it disturbs me that the letter was stolen. Who took it?"

D'Artagnan explained about the fight outside the inn at Calais. He also told the captain that he had last seen the gentleman who'd insulted his horse talking to the beautiful lady who'd kicked him.

"Did you mention my name to this gentleman

in connection with the letter?" asked Treville. "And did he have a scar on his cheek?"

"I did mention your name," said D'Artagnan. "And he did have a scar."

"That was Count de Rochefort," said Treville. "He's not a man you want to tangle with too often, if you value your life. He's Cardinal Richelieu's spy. He gathers information as others collect shells on a beach. Avoid him if you can. As for the lady, we have had reports of an English woman spying for the Cardinal. But who she is, I have no idea."

"I overheard them talking," said D'Artagnan.

"Perhaps you'll make a good spy one day," said Treville. "What were they talking about?"

D'Artagnan explained how the man had mentioned the Duke of Buckingham's name and how the woman was to follow his every move.

"Did he now," said Treville. "That is interesting. But remember, D'Artagnan, never mention the Duke's name in the King's presence. It'll be more than your life is worth."

Just then, D'Artagnan looked out of the window. To his astonishment, he saw the man he now knew to be Count de Rochefort.

D'Artagnan's temper got the better of him again. He ignored Treville's warning to keep away from the Cardinal's man. He wanted to give Rochefort a lesson for the cowardly act of putting his three men onto him.

"I apologize, sir," said D'Artagnan, before running off, "but honor calls. It's the man who stole my letter."

Without a further word, D'Artagnan raced out

of the room. He flew downstairs, taking four steps at a time. As he reached the bottom, he ran straight into one of the three musketeers who had been with Captain Treville just moments before.

"Get out of my way, sir!" cried D'Artagnan.

"You'd order *me* about, young idiot?" said the man. "You have a cheek to tell me, Athos, the boldest musketeer of them all, to get out of your way. That's an insult. Meet me in the palace courtyard tomorrow at noon. A little swordplay might teach you a lesson!"

"I will meet you, sir," promised D'Artagnan. "But now I must rush."

D'Artagnan raced away, only to bump into the second musketeer.

"You need some new eyes," said the man. "Bumping into me, Porthos, the boldest musketeer of them all, is not something a young fellow like you should do. I'll teach you a lesson. Meet me in the courtyard tomorrow, at one o'clock. I'll teach you some manners."

"I will meet you there," nodded D'Artagnan.

"But I must go now."

D'Artagnan hurried off, only to run straight into the third musketeer. This man was Aramis and he, too, demanded a sword fight. "Meet me in the courtyard tomorrow, at two o'clock!" he roared.

D'Artagnan finally got outside, only to find that Rochefort had vanished.

That night, as he fell asleep in a stable with his head resting on Methuselah's side, the three musketeers rode into his nightmares. To fight one was stupidity; to fight two, madness. To fight three certainly meant death.

D'Artagnan awoke in the darkness, with a start. "What am I worried about?" he said to himself, before drifting back to sleep. "If I am to due to die, at least it will be an honorable death at the hands of one of the King's Musketeers!"

Chapter 4

Fighting the Cardinal's Guards

D'Artagnan woke the next morning, utterly convinced that it was to be his last day on earth. If Athos didn't kill him, Porthos would. And if Porthos didn't, Aramis certainly would.

The hour of midday was striking when D'Artagnan reached the courtyard. Athos, who was already there, was still suffering from a wound received fighting with the Cardinal's men.

"My good arm is still not mended," he said. "I shall fight with my left hand. At least no one can say I used any advantage in killing such a young man."

"Then I shall use my left hand too," said D'Artagnan, proudly. "I'll not be accused of losing to a man who used his weaker arm."

Athos, surprised at the D'Artagnan's boldness, agreed. "You sound like a brave fellow," he smiled, starting to like the young man. "If I don't kill you this morning, I think we could be friends. Now, as soon as my two friends arrive, the duel can begin. They will make sure it is a fair contest."

Just then, Porthos and Aramis arrived.

"Don't kill the boy too quickly," said Porthos, a giant of a man. "I want to fight him next."

"And I don't want to fight a dead body either," said Aramis. "Leave a few bits of him that I can fight with."

"I could fight you all at the same time," said D'Artagnan, rather nervously. "Then you could all kill me."

"Good grief!" laughed Porthos. "It's a brave

man who is happy to fight three musketeers."

"No," said Athos to D'Artagnan. "I shall fight you first. And if you are still alive, then you can fight Porthos. And in the unlikely event that Porthos hasn't sat on you and squashed you to death, then Aramis shall have his chance."

"You humor me, gentlemen," said D'Artagnan. "You may regret it."

"Come then," said Athos. "Let's see your blade."

Poor D'Artagnan produced his broken sword.

"Ye Gods!" cried Porthos. "The boy was going to fight us with half a sword!"

"Here you are," said Aramis, throwing a spare sword he was carrying to D'Artagnan. "Borrow mine."

"On guard!" cried Athos.

The two men's swords had just touched to salute the coming fight, when a party of five of the Cardinal's men suddenly appeared. They included his best swordsmen, Jussac, Bernajoux, Bicarat, and Cahusac, all well-known to the three musketeers.

"Dueling is against the law," snapped Jussac. "Yet you devil-may-care, mustache-twisting, sword-clankers refuse to obey the law of the land."

"Leave us alone," growled Athos. "If we want to fight we shall, and you'll not tell us what we can or can't do!"

"In that case," said Jussac, "we'll have to arrest you all and throw you into the Bastille. A spell in there should silence you. Now make up your minds. Fight and face prison or go home quietly."

"It's five against three," whispered Athos, getting into a huddle with Porthos and Aramis. "We shall be killed for sure."

D'Artagnan heard what he said and stepped to their side. "It's five against four now," he said. "We shall not die if we fight together!"

"By the Lord, you'll make a fine musketeer one day," said Aramis, "but you're too young to die."

"I know I've not proved myself a true musketeer yet," said D'Artagnan, "but I feel I have the heart of a musketeer already."

Jussac was getting angry. "Make up your minds

now!" he shouted.

"We have," said Porthos.

D'Artagnan and the three musketeers rushed at the Cardinal's men. "On guard!" they bellowed as they met their five opponents.

Porthos took on Bicarat, an old enemy, while Athos went for Cahusac. Aramis found himself battling two of the Cardinal's men.

D'Artagnan came face-to-face with the men's leader, Jussac. Jussac was a great swordsman, the Cardinal's finest blade. Yet it required all his skill to defend himself from the young tiger, whose dashing and nimble feet were too quick for him.

Jussac became more and more frustrated that he could not strike the fast-moving youngster. At last, his patience exhausted, he sprang forwards, aiming a deadly thrust at D'Artagnan's heart.

The younger man parried Jussac's sword and struck home with his own sword. Jussac fell to the ground, badly wounded and unable to move another step.

D'Artagnan looked around to his friends.

Aramis had wounded one of his challengers and knocked him unconscious. Porthos and Bicarat, both injured, were still fighting. Athos had cut Cahusac quite a few times, although he too had been wounded, and now lay on the ground. Cahusac was about to strike Athos dead.

D'Artagnan leaped to Athos' defense, knocking the sword from Cahusac's hand and booting him across the courtyard like a leather ball.

Athos, still in agony from his wound, could not help laughing out loud. "Don't kill him," he said. "Monsieur Cahusac and I have an affair to settle. So leave him to fight another day."

The Cardinal's men saw their situation was hopeless. Taking their wounded, they hurried away, leaving D'Artagnan and his companions to celebrate their victory.

D'Artagnan felt so proud. "If I am not a musketeer yet," he said, "at least I have begun my apprenticeship."

"And so say all of us!" cried the others.

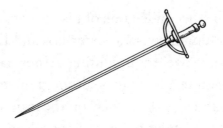

Chapter 5

D'Artagnan Falls in Love

News of the ferocious combat between the King's Musketeers and Richelieu's Guards soon spread around Paris.

Captain Treville scolded D'Artagnan and the three musketeers in public. But, in private, he congratulated them. He liked nothing better than to see his men give the Cardinal's bullies a bloody nose.

That evening King Louis paid Treville a visit.

"The Cardinal," he warned, "has been making complaints about your musketeers. Fighting again, I hear. Am I to hang these musketeers? Are they under your command or not?"

"They are under my command, Sire," replied Treville. "But they must not hang. On the contrary, they are good creatures, as meek as lambs, and have but one aim in life—to serve their King. But what are they to do? The Cardinal's guards are forever seeking quarrels with them."

"And is that what happened on this occasion?" asked the King.

"Indeed, Sire," replied Treville. "Three of your loyal musketeers whom you know well, Athos, Porthos, and Aramis, were attacked by five of the Cardinal's men. They had been talking to a young man named D'Artagnan who is in training to become a musketeer."

"Are you sure they didn't meet to duel with each other?" asked the King with a smile. "That's what my friend the Cardinal said."

"Never, sire. I believe they were discussing the flowers in the park when they were attacked most viciously. But of course, as you know, sometimes it is very difficult to get to the truth behind these affairs."

"You are right, Treville," said the King with another knowing smile. "But I hear that the young man under your command gave a good show of himself."

"Yes, sire," replied Treville. "D'Artagnan is little more than a boy, yet he has the heart of a lion. He was brutally attacked by Jussac but quite outfought him."

"But Jussac is one of the finest swordsmen in my kingdom," gasped the King.

"He found his master in young D'Artagnan," said Treville.

"Bring the boy to me tomorrow," said the King. "I want to see the man who put Jussac on his back."

***

At noon the next day, Athos, Porthos, Aramis, and D'Artagnan entered the King's Louvre Palace.

D'Artagnan bowed before the King.

"Why," said the King, "he is but a boy. And yet he floored Jussac."

"And helped me fight Cahusac too," said Athos.

The King took D'Artagnan aside. "I think you did well in defeating Jussac," he said. "But I must not upset the Cardinal too much. If you should fight Jussac again—if he ever recovers from the wound you gave him—be a little gentler with him. But remember this, young man; if the Cardinal asks me questions about you wounding Jussac,

I shall tell him you're an absolute devil and a rogue who should be hanged."

For the first time, D'Artagnan understood that the Cardinal was the true power behind the throne of King Louis XIII.

In the days ahead, the mustachioed threesome of Athos, Porthos, and Aramis became very fond of D'Artagnan, whose own mustache was growing bushier by the day. The four of them spent much of their time together.

D'Artagnan learned a lot about his three companions, and their servants.

Athos, some thirty years old, was the quietest of the three. He seldom spoke, but could fight like the devil. He had a world-weary sadness about him sometimes. His manservant, Grimaud, seldom spoke either, but the others guessed that he knew all his master's secrets.

Yet, there was one terrifying secret concerning Grimaud's master than neither he nor even Athos himself knew yet.

Porthos, in his mid-twenties, was simply the

loudest musketeer ever born. He talked loud and long, even if nobody was listening to him. He loved the sound of his own voice. He adored eating the finest foods and his clothing, which included a bright red cloak, was as loud as his character. Porthos' manservant was Mousqueton, a proud man who always insisted on dressing as smartly as his master, and eating as richly too.

Aramis, just twenty-three, was perhaps the kindest of the three musketeers. He always said that he never wanted to be a musketeer. His ambition was to enter the church. His man, Bazin, always wore a long black cloak. Bazin was waiting for the day when he would join his master in some great abbey.

D'Artagnan moved into an apartment in the same block as Athos, Porthos, and Aramis, and got himself a most able manservant named Planchet. Their apartment was near the Louvre Palace, and in a street where many royal attendants lived—including the beautiful Mademoiselle Bonacieux. Mademoiselle Bonacieux was one of the Queen's ladies-in-waiting. She lived with her uncle, Monsieur Bonacieux.

It didn't take long for the hot-blooded D'Artagnan to discover his beautiful neighbor, who had shining, jet-black hair and sparkling blue eyes. In truth, after meeting her, D'Artagnan announced to his fellow musketeers that he was in love for the first time in his life.

"Oh dear," chuckled Porthos, "we have a lovesick fool amongst us! He might as well throw his sword away for all the fighting he'll do now."

Aramis was more concerned. Like most musketeers, he knew of the dangers of becoming involved with anyone who was close to the Queen.

He took D'Artagnan aside one evening and explained the dangers. "The King and the Queen do not love each other. He is French. She is Spanish. They only married for political reasons to form an alliance between France and Spain. But they are just figureheads. And just so you know, it's hardly a secret that the Queen loves an Englishman, the Duke of Buckingham."

D'Artagnan was surprised to hear that name again so soon.

So that must be why the Count de Rochefort had asked Milady to follow the Duke!

Aramis continued with his warning. "The Queen involves her ladies-in-waiting in her intrigues with the Duke," he replied. "And the King becomes very angry at this. Even if he doesn't like the Queen, he doesn't like to be made a fool of by her activities.

"Already he has banished one lady-in-waiting from his court. She was lucky to escape with her head. Neither the King nor Cardinal Richelieu trusts the Queen, or her ladies-in-waiting."

"Well, I shall be proud to lose my head in the service of both Mademoiselle Bonacieux and her Queen," boasted D'Artagnan, already blinded by the power of his first love. "My sword is their sword! My life, their life!"

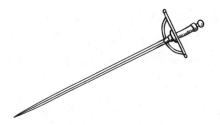

Chapter 6

On Milady's Trail

D'Artagnan's sword of honor, a cast-off given to him by Aramis, was needed a few nights later.

He heard cries coming from Mademoiselle Bonacieux's apartment. He rushed around and found her door had been forced open, and was now ajar. He saw that Mademoiselle Bonacieux was being interrogated by four of the Cardinal's black-cloaked officers.

"Mademoiselle," one of them was saying,

"a certain lady has told us that the Duke of Buckingham has arrived in Paris. Where is he? If you don't tell us, you'll spend the rest of your days in the Bastille."

D'Artagnan didn't hesitate. He raced through the doorway and into the room. With his sword twirling violently, he charged at the Cardinal's men. They took one look at the madman and flew from the room.

"At your service, Mademoiselle," said D'Artagnan, copying Porthos by making a small bow and twiddling his mustache.

"Ah, Monsieur," said the lady, who was perhaps the same age as D'Artagnan. "I can't thank you enough!"

"I have only done what any gentleman would do," replied D'Artagnan. "You owe me no thanks. But I'd like to know if I can help you in this matter of the Duke of Buckingham."

The lady was horrified to learn that her gallant helper knew the secret of the Duke. "*Never, never* utter his name again," she said. "The Cardinal's spies are everywhere. A mere mention of his name

will be the death of us all. Now, I am truly grateful
to you, but I must go."

"I'll come with you," offered D'Artagnan.
"You need protection. The Cardinal's men may
be waiting outside."

"It's too dangerous," she replied. "Now I must
hurry. And do not follow me. It could mean your
death. I'd never forgive myself if anything
happened to you."

D'Artagnan's heart melted as Mademoiselle
Bonacieux hurried out into the night, taking the
road toward the Louvre. He paused for a moment
and then, like a loyal puppy dog, he followed her,
always keeping just out of sight.

A little way on, D'Artagnan saw a tall
gentleman appear from the shadows. He spoke
briefly with Mademoiselle Bonacieux before they
both walked on toward the Louvre.

D'Artagnan followed them. A few moments
later another figure slipped out of the shadows,
also following the pair. A familiar scent wafted
into the air.

D'Artagnan, knowing it was Milady, hurried after her. Milady looked back and seemed to half-recognize her pursuer. She turned around and darted away down a lane, and vanished.

D'Artagnan ran to catch up with Mademoiselle Bonacieux and the man, who had turned a corner and disappeared. He had just reached the corner when the man suddenly leaped out at him.

"Young fellow," he said, "you're a dead 'un, unless you can explain why you are following us."

Somehow, D'Artagnan guessed that the man might be the Duke of Buckingham. But he wasn't sure. "I have sworn my life to guard and protect Mademoiselle Bonacieux," he replied. "And if she is in danger, you will have to fight me."

Just then Mademoiselle reappeared. "My dear Duke," she said. "Don't worry, it's D'Artagnan, who is training to be one of the King's Musketeers. He can be trusted."

"At your service, sir," said D'Artagnan.

"In that case," said the Duke, "follow a few

steps behind us and keep a lookout for any of the Cardinal's men or women."

"You were being followed by a woman," said D'Artagnan proudly. "I only know her as Milady."

"Good man!" said the Duke. "But next time, if you see her or anyone else following us, kill them instantly!"

D'Artagnan bowed to the Duke and drew his sword. "I shall be ready for anyone," he promised.

D'Artagnan followed the pair all the way to the Louvre. Reaching one of the outer walls, Mademoiselle Bonacieux picked up a small pebble and threw it against a window on the first floor.

The window opened and a rope tumbled down to the ground. The Duke gave Mademoiselle Bonacieux his deepest thanks and, with the agility of a monkey, climbed up the rope and into the palace.

D'Artagnan and Mademoiselle Bonacieux hurried home. The grateful lady allowed him to kiss her hand, before they parted.

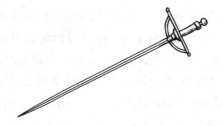

Chapter 7

The Duke and the Queen

Inside the Louvre, a lady-in-waiting led the Duke of Buckingham to the Queen's private quarters. The Queen appeared soon after. She was just twenty-five years old and was at the height of her beauty. The Duke, a year older, was as handsome as she was beautiful.

He kneeled down and kissed her hand. "Madame, it is an honor to see you again."

"Too dangerous an honor, my love," she replied,

beckoning him to stand up. "My spies tell me the Cardinal's men know you are in France. An English spy—a woman, I believe—followed you all the way from England but lost you in Paris. You should not have risked your life to come here. The Cardinal's men have vowed to kill you."

"My dear lady," said the Duke, "my life has been at your service since I first set eyes on you three years ago."

"We can never be together," sighed the Queen. "The King hates me, I know, but he is too proud to let me go."

"If you weren't the Queen of France, would you love me?" he asked.

"I need not answer that question," she replied, with a loving expression on her face. "We live in dangerous times. France will no doubt soon be at war with England. And you should know that all too well. Sometimes, I think the coming war is all about us. You will take England to war because of your love for me, and the Cardinal will take France to war because he hates both you and me."

The Duke certainly knew the dangerous

situation they were in. He was War Minister to Charles I, the King of England.

"Now," said the Queen, "however much I would like you to stay, you must return to England in all haste. We will meet again some happier day, I am sure."

The Queen reached for her jewelery box and took out a beautiful diamond brooch.

"It was a birthday present from the King," she said. "He didn't give it to me with love. I want you to have it as a token of my affection for you."

The Duke was overcome with gratitude. "I shall keep it by me always," he said.

***

Before dawn, the Duke left the palace by the same way he had entered. A horse was waiting for him and he galloped off on the road to Calais. From there he would sail to England.

If he had stayed a few minutes longer, he would have seen another of the Queen's ladies-in-waiting scurrying out of the main palace gate on her way to visit Cardinal de Richelieu. It was

Madame Lannoy. She had been with the Queen for many years . . . almost as many as she had been a spy for the Cardinal.

"The Duke of Buckingham has visited the Queen," she blurted out when the Cardinal was dragged from his bed to hear her news. "Even now he is on his way back to Calais, to get the boat for England."

"Blast the man!" snorted the Cardinal. "How did he get into the palace? He was supposed to be killed before he ever got there."

"Mademoiselle Bonacieux helped him," replied Madame Lannoy. "I saw her bring him to the palace. There was a young fellow who is often seen with the King's Musketeers, too. Unfortunately I don't know his name."

"I have a good idea who he might be," said the Cardinal, who had been informed of the arrival of the young trainee musketeer and his swordsmanship. "Now return to the palace and keep your ears and eyes open."

Madame Lannoy had one more piece of information. She told the Cardinal that the Queen

had given the Duke a present: the King's birthday brooch.

"Did she indeed," said the Cardinal, his eyebrows raised. "That information may be useful. Now be gone! I have important business to attend to with the Count de Rochefort."

As D'Artagnan had already discovered, the Count de Rochefort was the Cardinal's most trusted spy. And his business that day concerned a visit he intended to make to Mademoiselle Bonacieux's uncle.

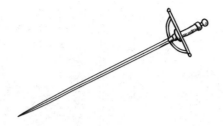

Chapter 8

A New Spy for the Cardinal

Monsieur Bonacieux was most surprised to find Count de Rochefort and the Cardinal's men knocking at his door before breakfast. They had come with an invitation he could not refuse. The Cardinal wanted to talk to him.

The terrified Monsieur Bonacieux was bundled into a wagon and driven off to see the great man. "What have I done wrong?" he cried as he was led before the Cardinal.

"Why nothing, my dear man," replied the Cardinal, with a deathly chill to his voice. "But you might be in trouble if you don't do something for me. You might even find yourself beneath the guillotine blade, waiting for it to drop. Or perhaps we could torture you for a week or two. But then again, if you do as you're told, nothing so horrible will happen to you. In fact, you could become rich by helping me."

That was a language Monsieur understood. He was not only a coward; he was a very greedy coward. "I have always been a Cardinal's man," he replied, knowing full well that he changed sides as many times as the wind changed directions. "I shall be proud to serve you."

"In that case," said the Cardinal, "I shall explain your new duties. Your niece, Mademoiselle Bonacieux, has been a mischievous girl. She is likely to lose her head very soon if she continues to plot and intrigue with the Queen. You can perhaps save her life by spying on her for me. I want to know everything she does. I want to hear about everyone she sees."

"She was always a troublesome thing," said Monsieur Bonacieux, for whom money always came before family concerns. "I shall gladly do the work."

"I see we shall soon become good friends," said the Cardinal, reaching into a drawer in his desk and producing a bag of gold coins. "And here is your first reward. Spend it wisely."

Monsieur Bonacieux took it gratefully.

"But remember, you are my man now!" said the Cardinal. "Cross me and I shall personally choose for you the most painful death ever suffered by man."

Monsieur Bonacieux, trembling from head to foot, scurried away to do his dirty work.

Meanwhile, the Cardinal continued to plot and he came up with a brilliant idea.

The Cardinal was a clever man and he could easily find an excuse to send the Queen to the Bastille. But he also knew the Queen was popular in France and the last thing that he, the Cardinal, wanted was to be blamed for removing her from her throne.

No, he wanted to make sure the King would be blamed if a way could be found to send the Queen to the Bastille. And the King would dearly love to find a reason to have his wife thrown into the Bastille for treason.

Knowing the King's birthday present to the Queen was now in the Duke of Buckingham's possession, the Cardinal planned a scheme involving the King's annual summer ball and the diamond brooch.

First, the Cardinal encouraged the King to persuade the Queen to wear her brooch at the ball. "It is such a lovely jewel," he said to the King, one day. "And the Queen always complains she has no chance to wear it. Her Majesty will be so proud to wear the brooch for you."

The King liked to keep the Cardinal happy. So he asked the Queen to make sure she wore the jewel at the ball.

The Queen could not refuse such a request, but after the King left, she almost fainted into the arms of Mademoiselle Bonacieux. "I am lost!" she cried. "How can I wear it when it's in England? That devilish Cardinal—this is his work! One of his spies must have told him that I had given the jewel away. Worse still, perhaps he knows that I gave it to the Duke of Buckingham."

Meanwhile, the Cardinal put the next part of his plan into operation. And that involved Milady, who was still in Paris. He sent a message to her, ordering her to visit him.

"Milady," he said when she arrived, "you failed me this time. You were asked to kill the Duke but you allowed, so I hear, a young swordsman to chase you off! Now I'm giving you the chance to make amends. I have a plot that will see the death of both the Queen and her loving English Duke. I want you to go to England and steal a little jewel from the Duke's house, and bring it to me."

The Cardinal was looking forward to the ball. It would be the night when he would expose the Queen by asking her why she wasn't wearing the brooch, right in front of the King. He would then produce the brooch himself, and reveal it had been in the Duke of Buckingham's possession.

"If the Queen is not in the Bastille before the last dance," he said to Milady, "then I'll give the King my palace."

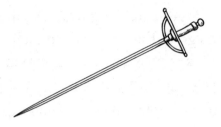

Chapter 9

Mademoiselle Bonacieux's Plan

In the Louvre, the Queen was desperately wondering what to do. Mademoiselle Bonacieux came up with a solution. "We must get the brooch back, and I know someone who'll do it for us."

She was thinking of her uncle. She didn't really trust him, but she knew he would do anything for money. She approached Monsieur Bonacieux and explained that she wanted someone to travel to England and bring back a diamond brooch. "The Queen will pay you well," she said.

Monsieur Bonacieux quickly realized that this would be a very tasty piece of information for the Cardinal. "The job is too dangerous," he told his niece. "I cannot do it."

"Perhaps there is another reason why you won't do it," she replied, suddenly seeing the bag of gold that the Cardinal had given him. "You seem to have come into money."

"It's just a reward for some work done for the King," he lied.

As soon as his niece had left, Bonacieux rushed to the Cardinal with his news.

The Cardinal knew he had to act quickly. He told Bonacieux to return home and wait for the Count de Rochefort to come and see him.

***

Meanwhile, Mademoiselle Bonacieux had another idea. Surely Monsieur D'Artagnan would go to England for her and bring back the brooch.

"It's a glorious mission," he cried excitedly, when she asked him. "When do I go?"

"You must be ready to ride later tonight," she

said. "And remember, you have the Queen's life in your hands on this mission."

"And may I take my friends Athos, Porthos, and Aramis with me?"

"You'll need them," said Mademoiselle Bonacieux. "This is the most dangerous journey you'll make in your life. If the Cardinal gets to hear about it, then his men will be looking for you everywhere. Capture means certain death."

"We will need money," said D'Artagnan.

Mademoiselle Bonacieux said she would find money somehow. She suddenly thought of her uncle, and the money she had seen in his apartment.

She hurried upstairs and was about to enter Bonacieux's apartment when she heard two people talking inside the door. It was Bonacieux and the Count de Rochefort, who had been asked by the Cardinal to go to England, to help Milady and make sure the Queen's agents didn't get hold of the brooch.

Rochefort now wanted to see if Bonacieux had

any other information, before he left for England.

"All my niece said to me," explained Monsieur Bonacieux, "was that she wanted someone to go to England and get this brooch for the Queen."

"Now we see the treachery of the Queen and her ladies," said Rochefort.

Mademoiselle Bonacieux was horrified, as she listened outside the door. She bit her tongue to stop herself from crying out, "Traitorous uncle!"

Just then, she heard the two men coming to the door. She hid herself behind a curtain.

"Keep your eyes open while I am gone, Bonacieux," said Rochefort.

"Count, do you think I should ask the Cardinal for more money, for the information I've given him?" asked Bonacieux as Rochefort raced down the stairs.

"You can try," Rochefort called back. "But don't take the Cardinal's money too easily. He never forgives anyone if they fail him. I should know because it is always me who has to kill his enemies. I strangle them, usually."

Monsieur Bonacieux shivered as never before, but he still left the house to ask the Cardinal for more money.

As soon as he had gone, Mademoiselle Bonacieux dashed into the room and stole her uncle's bag of gold. It would be more than enough to fund D'Artagnan's journey to London.

A little later, D'Artagnan, now astride Methuselah and with the gold safely in his saddlebag, went to see Captain Treville. He wanted the captain's permission for Athos, Porthos, Aramis, and himself to set out on a mission of national importance. "I am sworn to secrecy," he said, "but we'll be going on the Queen's service."

Treville, who was very fond of the Queen, gave his permission immediately. But he gave a warning. "If it's the Queen's business, it's always possible you'll come across two of her greatest enemies."

"Do you mean Milady and the Count de Rochefort?" asked D'Artagnan.

"I do," replied Treville. "Those two are more dangerous than a pair of tigers and more vicious than hungry polecats."

It was almost midnight by the time D'Artagnan and his man Planchet, together with the three musketeers, set off for London.

As they passed Monsieur Bonacieux's apartment, they heard a dreadful howl coming from the window. Monsieur Bonacieux had just discovered that someone had stolen his gold!

Chapter 10

All for One, One for All!

"And why the devil are we going to London?" grumbled Porthos, still half asleep.

"I cannot say yet, but Captain Treville has given his permission for this important task," answered D'Artagnan. "It's a death or glory mission."

"Death or glory?" asked Porthos.

With a frown on his face, D'Artagnan added, "It's death, I think. I'm not sure we will all get to London."

"What do you mean?" asked Aramis.

"I mean it is a mission of the most dangerous kind," replied D'Artagnan. "One or more of us may be killed on the road to London."

"Well, if I'm going to die," said Porthos, "I'd like to know what cause I'm going to die for."

Athos wasn't so bothered. "If our young friend says we go with Captain Treville's blessing, so be it. Let's all go and get killed, wherever we're told to go. All for one, one for all, say I!"

"It might help," laughed Aramis, "if D'Artagnan had bought a faster horse for the journey. We probably won't reach Calais before next Christmas!"

D'Artagnan laughed in return. "Methuselah will get me there, and alive, I hope."

So the four companions rode on. But they soon found themselves in trouble!

A mile or two out of Paris, they were attacked by some ruffians. Heavily outnumbered, the four managed to get away in the end. But Porthos, who had been knocked unconscious, was left behind in a monastery to recover.

A few miles on, Aramis was hit by a musket ball fired by a drunken farmer outside an inn. He was carried off to have the ball removed from his shoulder.

D'Artagnan, Athos, and Planchet rode on. On entering the town of Amiens, Athos was attacked by wild dogs and fell from his horse. He was left at an inn to recover from his wounds.

Still D'Artagnan would not abandon his mission for his beloved Mademoiselle Bonacieux. He and Planchet rode slowly on.

It was midday by the time they reached Calais and discovered that the Cardinal had issued special orders to the harbormaster. No one was to board a ship for England unless they had a pass signed by him.

D'Artagnan and Planchet retired to the local inn to find stabling for their horses and discuss what they should do next. D'Artagnan saw that Rochefort and his servant Lubin were already there. No doubt they would soon board a ship for England.

The two men overheard Rochefort and Lubin talking about their traveling passes. That gave D'Artagnan an idea. He was far too noble a character to think of stealing someone else's property, but he looked at Planchet with a knowing smile. Planchet was the man for the job. He knew exactly what his master was thinking.

With Rochefort and Lubin looking the other way, it only took Planchet a split second to spirit away Rochefort's traveling bag, two seconds to remove the travel passes, and one second to return the bag.

"Quick!" shouted D'Artagnan, once they were outside. "There's a ship about to leave!"

The harbormaster, who had no idea what Rochefort or Lubin looked like, examined their passes. "It seems the Cardinal is anxious to stop someone from crossing to England," he said. "But your passes are all in order. Go aboard."

D'Artagnan and Planchet, for the time being under the identity of Count Rochefort and his manservant Lubin, leaped aboard just in time.

As the boat left the quay, D'Artagnan shouted back to the harbormaster. "There are two men sitting by the fire at the inn, who are wanted by Cardinal de Richelieu for robbery and murder. Have them arrested and sent back to the Bastille! I, Count de Rochefort, will reward you when I return."

"I will do all you ask, sir," replied the harbormaster. "And what are their names?"

"D'Artagnan and his manservant Planchet," shouted D'Artagnan, against the wind. "They are dangerous men. Use all the force you have!"

D'Artagnan and Planchet were still laughing as the coastline of France disappeared into the distance.

Back in France, Rochefort and Lubin had received several nasty wounds in a violent sword fight with the harbormaster's men. They were eventually overcome, arrested, and sent back to Paris in chains. They were only released after the Cardinal himself identified the pair.

The Cardinal wasn't surprised when Rochefort, swearing death and destruction on his enemies, named D'Artagnan and Planchet as the men responsible for their arrests.

As he ordered Rochefort and Lubin to set out again for England immediately, a cruel smile crossed his face. "This man D'Artagnan is becoming a nuisance," he said to himself. "He'll have to be watched carefully."

Chapter 11

To England

On arriving in Dover on England's south coast, D'Artagnan hired horses for himself and Planchet, and immediately set off for the Duke of Buckingham's country estate. It was only a few miles from Dover.

It was late evening by the time they reached the Duke's house. A servant answered the door and D'Artagnan was quickly shown into his presence. He explained to the Duke why the Queen desperately needed the diamond brooch she had given him.

"The Cardinal will have her accused of treason," said D'Artagnan, "if she doesn't have it for the King's summer ball. And that's just three days away."

"If she needs the jewel, noble D'Artagnan," said the Duke, "then she must have it."

He hurried away and brought back the box that contained the brooch. "I shall keep it under lock and key until you leave," he said, after showing it to D'Artagnan.

The Duke then sent word to Dover for an English naval ship to be made ready to take D'Artagnan, Planchet, and the brooch safely back to France the next morning.

That night, D'Artagnan was so anxious to return to France that he hardly slept a wink. He was still wide awake in the early hours of the morning, when he heard the sound of breaking glass. He got up, and still in his nightclothes, crept downstairs.

Someone was in the Duke's study,

rummaging though his desk. D'Artagnan tiptoed through the door and saw the shadowy figure of a lady, with a candlestick in her hand.

She turned, and suddenly saw D'Artagnan. Their eyes met. A look of half recognition crossed D'Artagnan's face. The flickering candlelight was too gentle to show the woman's face in detail. But that didn't prevent him from identifying his thief. She was wearing the same expensive and unmistakable perfume. It was Milady!

For a moment neither moved, but watched each other like a cat and mouse. Even D'Artagnan,

young and brave as he was, was hypnotized as the shadowy light gave him occasional glances of her beautiful, yet cruel gaze.

"We have met before, Mademoiselle," said D'Artagnan at last.

"I don't know you, young man," lied the woman. "We have never met."

"Oh, yes we have," said D'Artagnan. "At Calais some time ago. You were with Count de Rochefort."

"I know no such man," snapped the woman.

"We met again when I caught you following the Duke in Paris," continued D'Artagnan.

"Impossible!" she replied in a voice that sounded more like that of a hissing snake than a human.

Then, without another word, she struck a vicious blow at D'Artagnan with the candlestick, giving him a nasty cut on the head.

D'Artagnan grabbed Milady by the shoulders and threw her to the ground. She was up in a flash, scratching at his eyes and kicking him.

D'Artagnan landed on his back on the floor, with the crazed woman still clawing at his eyes. Then she was gone; leaping out of the broken window and vanishing into the night.

The noise awoke the Duke, who now appeared beside D'Artagnan. The Duke thought that D'Artagnan must have been attacked by an animal. His face was clawed and bleeding.

D'Artagnan got to his feet. "It's nothing, sir," he said. "I shall have my revenge on the woman who did this, but she didn't escape with the Queen's brooch."

"I thank you, young man, for saving the jewel," said the Duke.

The Duke then unlocked a secret drawer in his desk, picked out the brooch, and handed it to D'Artagnan. "It is time for you to leave," he said. "The sooner you return the jewel to the Queen, the better."

The Duke's coach was prepared and D'Artagnan and Planchet set off for Dover harbor.

At Dover, as promised by the Duke, a naval

vessel was waiting for them. They quickly boarded the ship and set sail.

As the ship left the harbor entrance, another boat entered. It was a French vessel, and hanging on the side rail of it were Rochefort and Lubin. They looked up at the bigger ship and in the light of the rising sun, saw D'Artagnan and Planchet.

Rochefort's curse echoed through the chill, early morning air.

***

By that evening D'Artagnan and Planchet had gotten ashore near Calais, carefully avoiding the Cardinal's extra guards, who were now watching the harbor. They collected their horses from the stable and rode back toward Paris.

D'Artagnan and Planchet arrived back in Paris on the eve of the King's ball. The talk in town was all about Count de Rochefort and Lubin being arrested in Calais, and sent back in chains to Paris. There was also much gossip about the gold robbery from Monsieur Bonacieux's apartment!

How D'Artagnan laughed, but he guessed

there might be a price to pay for humiliating the Cardinal's men.

D'Artagnan ran to the Louvre, where the grateful Mademoiselle Bonacieux led him into the Queen's private quarters. The Queen was much relieved to have the brooch safe again. Mademoiselle Bonacieux's personal reward to D'Artagnan was to allow him to kiss her hand again. It just made him love her even more.

Then she asked D'Artagnan where the other musketeers were.

"Injured, abed, or waiting for their heads to mend," laughed D'Artagnan. "Nothing serious. They got into some trouble on the road to Calais. They are still scattered around France recovering from some noble wounds received in service of their Queen. They'll be back soon."

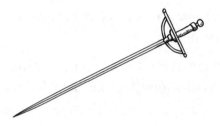

Chapter 12

The King's Ball

The Queen gave D'Artagnan and Mademoiselle Bonacieux a special invitation to the King's ball.

Everyone was there, including the Cardinal and a still furious Rochefort. The Count had just returned from his failed mission to England, and would have dearly loved to have run D'Artagnan through with his sword. But that wasn't the sort of behavior allowed within the strict rules of the court.

Spying was a deadly game. But the cloak and dagger world of the Cardinal's spies and agents was temporarily suspended for events such as the King's ball. The world returned to normal for a while.

Even so, the atmosphere was heavy with intrigue and menace in the Louvre that night. D'Artagnan was well aware that the Cardinal's cruel but always smiling eyes were staring at him.

Captain Treville, who was also there, had another warning for D'Artagnan. "Remember," he said, "you must look out for yourself. The Cardinal may beam and smile at you, yet will happily have you murdered by his executioner, the cruel Rochefort, at the drop of a guillotine blade. He wouldn't shed a tear if the Queen or her lady-in-waiting, Mademoiselle Bonacieux, should die in mysterious circumstances."

But nothing was going to stop D'Artagnan from enjoying himself that night. He smiled to himself when he saw the Queen, with the diamond brooch pinned to her beautiful ball gown. And he danced with his darling

Mademoiselle all night.

The next morning, D'Artagnan received a note from Mademoiselle Bonacieux, asking him to meet her in the Louvre Palace gardens. The young man ran all the way there. At first, he couldn't see her. Then a scuffle in a distant corner of the gardens caught his eye. Someone was being dragged into a carriage against their will. It was a woman.

D'Artagnan recognized the color of the woman's dress. It was Mademoiselle Bonacieux and she was being kidnapped! By the time he had raced across to the scene, the carriage was rattling away into the distance in a cloud of dust.

Kidnapped! D'Artagnan knew it must be the Cardinal's men who had Mademoiselle Bonacieux. He was horrified. He ran to Captain Treville and asked what could be done.

"We are just servants of the Cardinal, and the King and the Queen," the captain explained. "We cannot interfere with what they and their spies and ministers do. We can only hope for the best."

D'Artagnan set off for home, a very unhappy

And what a sword fight it was!

"I could fight you all at the same time,"
said D'Artagnan, rather nervously.

"Quick!" shouted D'Artagnan, once they were outside.
"There's a ship about to leave!"

"I am training to be a musketeer and sworn
to serve the King," answered D'Artagnan.

Four muskets blasted out.

"You killed a dummy, madam," replied the Duke.

D'Artagnan, Athos, Porthos, and Aramis had already raced there and hidden themselves in the trees above the crossroads.

All four musketeers whipped out their swords, swishing them through the air just an inch or two from Monsieur Bonacieux's nose.

man. He promised himself that he would never leave his apartment again without being armed with sword and pistol. Nor would he cease the hunt to find Mademoiselle Bonacieux.

D'Artagnan knew he was in real danger from the Cardinal and his men. In his mind, he listed all the things he had done which might bring a speedy and bloody revenge.

First, he had helped Mademoiselle Bonacieux escape from the Cardinal's inquisitors, and then he had prevented Milady from assassinating the Duke of Buckingham. More recently, he had made an absolute fool of Rochefort and Lubin, and foiled the Cardinal and Milady's plot to steal the Queen's diamond brooch.

That night D'Artagnan was cheered to see that Athos, Porthos, and Aramis had all returned. And what a sight they were! Athos and Porthos were covered in bandages. Aramis had his arm in a sling.

"Welcome back, my friends!" cried D'Artagnan. "You've no idea how much I have missed you. And how much I need you now."

D'Artagnan explained all that had happened in London, Calais, and Paris.

"I care not for my own life anymore," he said. "The Cardinal, Rochefort, and Milady can do to me what they like now. All I want to do is find Mademoiselle Bonacieux."

"We'll find her," said Athos. "I promise."

"Indeed, we will," said Porthos.

"Yes, my brave friends," said Aramis. "All for one, one for all!"

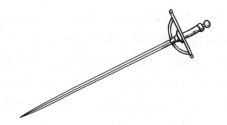

Chapter 13

A First Clue to Milady's Identity

D'Artagnan did all he could to find news of Mademoiselle Bonacieux, but the Cardinal's men had covered all their tracks. She had disappeared into thin air.

The young swordsman was now often to be found lurking in the area around the Cardinal's palace at night, hoping to see or overhear something.

There was one particular house in the area that D'Artagnan paid special attention to. It was a house with the address, No. 6, Place Royale. D'Artagnan always thought of the place as rather sinister, because it was used as a lodging house for people visiting the Cardinal.

One night, D'Artagnan was hiding in a hedge when two people emerged from the door of No. 6. Peering between the branches, he immediately recognized Count de Rochefort. He was talking with a woman. The waft of perfume told D'Artagnan that Milady was back in Paris. To his horror, D'Artagnan discovered they were talking about his own early death!

"I want D'Artagnan dead," Rochefort was saying, "whether the Cardinal gives permission or not. He's a danger to us, and the Cardinal."

"I wish I'd killed him in England," replied Milady. "He won't get a second chance to make a fool of me. I cannot understand why the Cardinal still refuses to have him killed. He's an enemy of the Cardinal and has proved it a hundred times over. So have those playmates of his, Athos,

Porthos, and Aramis. Let's be done with them all. Half a dozen guards, a dark night . . . and we could cut all their throats!"

"I agree," said Rochefort. "But the Cardinal thinks he might be able to use D'Artagnan. With persuasion, he thinks he might join us. That's why he wants them all kept alive for now."

"By the way," said Milady, "my former brother-in-law, the English ambassador, Lord de Winter, has arrived in town for negotiations with the King. Just remember, he has no idea I work for the Cardinal and France."

Milady suddenly started laughing hysterically. "I don't think Lord de Winter likes me very much. I married his brother, swindled him out of the entire de Winter family fortune, and then killed him once I'd gotten it!"

D'Artagnan wasn't surprised to hear how cheap life was to Milady. But he was astonished to hear that she had been the sister-in-law of an English lord. "At last!" he thought. "I now have my first clue to the true identity of Milady."

Just after D'Artagnan got home that evening,

Porthos burst in to say that he had been arguing with an English lord and three of his friends. "They have demanded a sword fight with me and three of my friends," he said.

"All for one, one for all," said D'Artagnan. "A fight will clear the brain of all my worldly worries. When and where do we fight?"

"On the terrace behind the Louvre at six o'clock tomorrow evening," replied Porthos.

With possible war approaching, they saw it as a good chance to strike the first blow for France.

***

The four English swordsmen gathered on the terrace that evening to face Athos, Porthos, Aramis, and D'Artagnan. Each man had brought his own manservant with him.

The English were all men of high rank, and when they saw the four humble French swordsmen they were disappointed at the opposition.

"We are all lords," moaned one. "Why should we fight such lowly creatures?"

"I agree," said a second. "But perhaps we can do our King a favor."

"How's that?" asked the third.

"It won't matter much, I suppose," replied the second Englishman, "but to kill four Frenchmen now would save the bother when the war breaks out."

Porthos exploded with anger. He pulled out his sword and twirled it in the face of the first man. Athos did the same with the second man. Aramis leaped at the third Englishman with such violence

that his enemy had to retreat to collect himself.

D'Artagnan walked calmly up to the fourth man and tickled the tip of his nose with the point of his sword. "On guard, Englishmen!" he cried.

"On guard, Frenchmen!" was the reply.

Immediately eight swords glittered in the rays of the setting sun, and the combat began.

It was war. Each man was fighting for his country.

Chapter 14

The Fleur-de-Lis

Athos fenced with his usual calmness, almost as if he was practicing at fencing school; always darting and diving, always out of reach of his enemy's sword. He'd promised to kill his man with one blow. He didn't like anyone to suffer.

Porthos, as would be expected, was fighting like a man possessed. His opponent was already in retreat.

Aramis, the poet of the four, fought with speed.

He was thinking how he had a poem to finish that night.

D'Artagnan's opponent was his equal. They fought blow for blow.

Athos took first blood and killed his man with a single blow to the heart. Porthos struck next with a slashing blow to the thigh of his opponent. The second Englishman fell to the ground, unable to rejoin the fight. Porthos, ever the gentleman, picked him up and carried him back to his carriage to be looked after by his manservant.

Aramis found he had a coward on his hands. He retreated and retreated until he ended up hiding under his own carriage. Aramis returned to watch D'Artagnan. The young trainee musketeer was already fighting as if it was only a matter of time before he ended the fight, despite his opponent's skill.

He was right. D'Artagnan caught his opponent a glancing blow to the shoulder. The man tumbled to the ground, clasping his wound. D'Artagnan sprang forward and stood astride him, his sword pointing at his throat.

"I could kill you, my lord," he said. "You are at my mercy, but I shall spare you your life. Your name, sir?"

"I am Lord de Winter, Ambassador to King Charles I of England. I reluctantly yield to you."

D'Artagnan was astonished to hear the name again. "Excuse me, sir," said D'Artagnan. "You have a sister-in-law, I believe."

"It pains me to admit it," he said. "I am too much of a gentleman to talk of that infamous creature, other than to say she was my sister-in-law once. She was married to my brother whom she killed for his money, but no one could prove it. So she escaped with her life. Please don't ask me any more about her."

Bit by bit, D'Artagnan was learning more and more about the monstrous Milady.

He helped Lord de Winter back to his carriage, while Athos, Porthos, and Aramis carried the other men to their carriages. D'Artagnan was just about to rejoin his companions when Milady appeared.

"I watched your fight, Monsieur D'Artagnan," she said, an evil smile twisting her lips. "Kill when you have the chance, young man. Never give mercy. Mercy always comes back to haunt you."

Milady's smile chilled D'Artagnan's heart and sent shudders down his spine.

She smiled wickedly at him again and began to walk away. Then she turned back and said, "Monsieur D'Artagnan. We will meet again, I promise!"

She turned away once more but suddenly, she cried out as if she had been injured.

D'Artagnan saw that the shoulder of her dress had caught on a thorn bush. For the briefest moment, her left shoulder was bared and D'Artagnan saw something. He had the distinct impression it was a tattoo showing a little flower called a Fleur-de-Lis.

Someone else saw that Fleur-de-Lis. Athos had reappeared. He was now staring in disbelief at both the Fleur-de-Lis, which he recognized instantly, and the face of the woman who bore that flower!

Athos knew it was no ordinary tattoo. The Fleur-de-Lis had been branded on that shoulder. It was the hangman's mark. The Fleur-de-Lis was branded on all French prisoners sentenced to death.

Athos' face had turned as pale as could be. And that was no surprise. The last time he had seen the woman, she was hanging from a gallows!

Just then, Milady caught sight of Athos. She let out an awful shriek. It was as if she had seen a ghost. She raced away, adjusting her dress to hide the mark from Athos' astonished eyes.

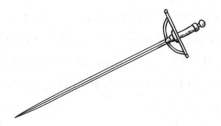

Chapter 15

War with England

The next day D'Artagnan received an invitation to call on Cardinal de Richelieu.

From the conversation he had overheard between Rochefort and Milady, D'Artagnan knew the Cardinal wasn't going to hang him yet. He guessed the all-powerful man was going to try to recruit him.

When D'Artagnan was ushered into the great man's chamber, the Cardinal was all smiles—even if they were false ones.

"I have heard much of you, D'Artagnan," he said. "You are obviously a brave young man, but I have learned that you have many enemies. If you do not change your ways, they will kill you for sure."

"I'm sure they will," replied D'Artagnan, looking the Cardinal closely in the eye. "Yet, I am but one and they are many. And they have important supporters in high places."

The cardinal ignored the remark and continued. "You too could have a friend in a high place," he said. "I have an offer to make. I would like you and your three friends to join my Guards. What say you to that?"

"I am training to be a musketeer and sworn to serve the King," answered D'Artagnan immediately. "I cannot leave the King, especially in these dangerous times with England almost at war with us."

The Cardinal was annoyed at the answer. "You should know, D'Artagnan," he said, "that I have had many serious complaints against you. Dueling in public places, dabbling in the Queen's affairs, and even robbing my own man, Rochefort, of his passes to England.

"These are all serious offenses that might take you to the Bastille. If you won't join me, your life will be in even more danger than it is now. I will have to withdraw my protection. And the lives of you and your musketeer friends will be worth nothing without it. Now get out of my sight and give some serious thought to my offer. It will be my last."

D'Artagnan thought he had never seen a more frightening look on the face of a human being. But then he thought of Milady. Her murderous eyes made the Cardinal's look as gentle as a baby's.

As he left the Cardinal's palace, D'Artagnan saw Milady talking with two ruffians. He saw her point to him, as though making sure they could recognize him again.

***

Athos had thought of telling his fellow musketeers that he had recognized Milady, but decided against it for now. He wanted to keep it a very close secret.

Another reason was that news had reached Paris that an English army had invaded the west coast of France and captured and occupied the main naval port of La Rochelle.

All talk of the search for Mademoiselle Bonacieux and the identity of Milady was forgotten as both the Cardinal's Guards and the King's Musketeers were ordered to the coast to lay siege to the English army.

Before the King's Musketeers left for the coast, Captain Treville called D'Artagnan to his office and promoted him from a trainee, to a full musketeer. "You are a better swordsman than most," said Treville. "And a braver young fellow I have never met."

Bursting with pride, D'Artagnan could not wait to tell his three companions. But it seemed they already knew, for when he returned to his apartment, he found them all there waiting for him. And they had bought him a present—a brand new uniform of the King's Musketeers!

The war between England and France wasn't

so much a war, as a battle of hearts. The Duke of Buckingham wanted a war against the French because among the spoils of victory would be the Queen of France, the love of his life. The Cardinal also wanted war because it might bring about the death of the Duke of Buckingham.

But for D'Artagnan and his fellow musketeers, the battle to come was all about fame and glory.

When they arrived at the battle front, the four musketeers and their comrades found themselves in deep trenches that had been dug around the town of La Rochelle. The trenches were used to get close to the town walls without being seen.

One morning, the four friends were ordered to the front line to spy out enemy defenses. With their bodies bent double to avoid enemy fire, they set off. Almost instantly D'Artagnan felt a musket shot fizz past his right ear. A second shot whistled right through his hat. A third shot grazed the back of his neck.

The shots were not coming from the enemy. They had been fired from behind him. It was clear they were no accident. D'Artagnan looked back and saw two soldiers with smoking muskets running off. He raced after them.

The assassins were quickly caught. D'Artagnan recognized them as the two men who had been with Milady when she pointed at him in Paris. Both pleaded for mercy.

"We were ordered to kill you!" cried one.

"Who gave the order?" shouted D'Artagnan.

"It was a young lady who was with Count de Rochefort," said the other. "She sent us to kill you."

D'Artagnan knew how lucky he was to still be alive. He was a marked man, and Milady would stop at nothing to kill him, even in the middle of a war!

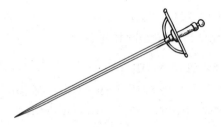

Chapter 16

The Confessions of Athos

A few days later, D'Artagnan was surprised to receive a case of wine from a man named Godeau. He was a wine grower who often supplied the King's Musketeers with his produce. With the wine came a short note:

> *A small gift for you and your fellow musketeers who are fighting so proudly for France. Godeau.*

D'Artagnan arranged to have a special dinner so that all his musketeer friends could enjoy the wine. It was never to take place. A rogue soldier stole one of the bottles of wine. A few hours later, he was found dead—poisoned. The wine hadn't come from Godeau. Milady had sent it.

"Poisoned wine!" D'Artagnan said to his three friends. "That evil woman will try to kill me any way she can."

Athos stepped forward. "My brothers," he said, "it's time I revealed a terrible secret to you all. It's a secret that should have stayed with the dead. But someone from the past has come back to haunt me. It concerns the woman D'Artagnan knows as Milady. And I don't think it's just D'Artagnan she wants to murder. It's all of us. I want to tell you about the woman. She was my wife!"

Athos' three companions stared in disbelief as he continued.

"We were married when we were both very young. I came from a rich family and it didn't take that dreadful creature long to steal a fortune in priceless jewels from my parents. She always said

that it was the servant girls in the house who stole them. My parents must have discovered that she was the guilty one because a few days later I found them dead. That woman murdered them to hide the truth."

"Did she escape punishment?" asked D'Artagnan.

"No," said Athos. "My mother kept a diary and she had written about how she thought my wife was the guilty one. They found the jewels in the woman's apartment. She was arrested, tried, and sentenced to hang. I witnessed the hangman branding her with the Fleur-de-Lis."

"But she's alive, so she can't have been hanged," said a puzzled Aramis.

"She was hanged," replied Athos. "I saw the hangman pull the lever that opened the trapdoor beneath her feet. I saw her disappear. I saw the rope twist and turn. And from that day to this, I thought her dead. She has come back from the dead to haunt me."

D'Artagnan, Porthos, and Aramis were silent for a while, almost too shocked to speak.

"Someone must have been waiting below the trap door," said Aramis at last.

"Someone must have cut her down before she died," nodded Porthos.

"What does it matter?" sighed Aramis. "All I want now is to see her dead. And she won't be easy to kill, either. It's us or her this time. Shortly after I saw her branded with the Fleur-de-Lis, she swore to kill any man who saw that brand. Evil though she is, even she felt the shame of it."

"And her true name?" asked D'Artagnan.

"Anne de Brueil," replied Athos. "And she was a French woman, not English as many thought. That was the name of the woman whom I saw hanged on the gallows. And that is still the name of the woman, as far as I am concerned."

"The witch!" cried D'Artagnan. "I know some more about her too. She must have married again because Lord de Winter told me he had been her brother-in-law. She had murdered his brother. So she has already killed three people and no doubt many more that we haven't heard about."

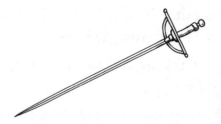

Chapter 17

The Red Dovecot Inn

Later that night, the four musketeers were off duty and walking in the countryside behind the French lines.

"Come on," said D'Artagnan. "All this talk of murder and mayhem has made me thirsty. Let's go and find an inn and share a drink. All for one, one for all!"

"The Red Dovecot Inn is not far away," said Porthos. "Live well while we may. That's what

I say. For tomorrow we may be Milady's latest victims . . . or rather, Anne de Brueil's."

They found the inn and, seating themselves by the fire, called for drinks.

D'Artagnan was warming his hands when he caught the faintest whiff of a familiar perfume. There was an old disused stove pipe that went up beside the chimney. And that was where the fragrance was coming from.

D'Artagnan looked up the pipe and heard voices. A man and a woman were talking in the room above. He could clearly hear their words echoing down the pipe.

It didn't take him long to guess who the talkers were. He froze for a moment and then pointed up the chimney, whispering two names to his friends: "Milady and the Cardinal!"

The four musketeers leaned forward to listen.

"No doubt the Duke of Buckingham will soon tire of this battle," Cardinal Richelieu was saying. "And then I will have my revenge against him. I want him killed. Could it be done without me—

we, I mean—being suspected?"

"It can," Milady replied. "And it shall be done as soon as possible. I shall see to it myself. Now in return, will you grant me a favor . . . the death of those four annoying musketeers, D'Artagnan and his friends?"

"But, if my intelligence is correct," said the Cardinal, "you have already tried twice to murder one or other of them recently."

"It's true," Milady admitted, "but it will be easier if I have your personal authority."

"It is not easy for a Cardinal to authorize a murder," said the Cardinal.

"But how many of your men have they killed?" she asked.

"It's true, they have killed my men in sword fights," he replied. "Perhaps the Duke's life for the four musketeers is a fair exchange. Give me some paper and pen and ink, and I'll write you an authorization to kill the four. In any case, they had the chance to join my guards and they turned me down. I warned D'Artagnan I couldn't protect them anymore."

"And what if my former brother-in-law, Lord de Winter, comes to meet his death too?"

"I can ignore such a murder," said the Cardinal. "He's an Englishman. One more dead Englishman will help our cause while the war continues. I will give you a death warrant for all six men: the Duke, the four musketeers, and Lord de Winter."

There was no more speaking for a while, but the four musketeers could just hear the scratching of a quill pen on rough paper.

"There!" said the Cardinal. "Now you have it. You may kill the six in my name. They are murders you can never be hanged for."

D'Artagnan was horrified at the cold-blooded nature of both Milady and the Cardinal. Athos had to be restrained from leaping up the stairs and killing the pair there and then.

"Don't be a fool," said Aramis. "Kill the Cardinal and we'll be on the end of a rope by tomorrow morning. No. We must bide our time. We must strike when the Cardinal cannot protect her."

Soon after, the musketeers heard a door above them open. They scurried across the room to hide in a dark corner, and watched as the Cardinal came downstairs and left the inn.

They waited for a while and then left the inn themselves. Back at camp, D'Artagnan, Porthos, and Aramis retired to their tents to sleep. They assumed Athos had done the same.

But just at that moment he was galloping back to the inn.

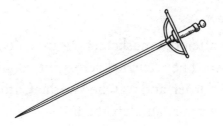

Chapter 18

Athos and Anne de Brueil

Athos reached the Red Dovecot Inn and hurried inside. Throwing his dark cloak around him and pulling his hat down over his eyes, he swiftly climbed the stairs and burst into Milady's room.

Milady turned around and saw the dark shadow that had just entered. "Who are you?" she gasped. "What do you want?"

"So it truly is you," said Athos, removing his cloak and hat, and drawing a loaded pistol from

his belt. "I too have returned to haunt you. I thought you dead all these years."

"It's true, I did fall through the gallows trapdoor," said Milady. "I thought I was dead. But I did not know that someone was beneath, waiting to catch me. It was easy to slip away through the crowds after that."

"And the man's name?" growled Athos.

"Count de Rochefort," she answered.

"I might have known it," said Athos. "Two devils together."

Milady stared at Athos. She wondered if he was about to shoot her.

"You have done so much wrong," continued Athos. "Nothing can remove the bloody stains on your soul, nor the brand the hangman burned into your shoulder. Even now you have the Cardinal's death warrant for more murders."

"What do you want of me?" Milady asked nervously.

"I have a warning to give you," said Athos. "The Duke of Buckingham and Lord de Winter are Englishmen, and we are at war with England. If they die, so be it. But my fellow musketeers are friends and comrades whom I'll defend to the death. Touch a hair of their heads and I swear that I shall send you back to hell before you can take another breath."

Athos cocked his pistol, ready to fire it. Milady sat motionless as Athos slowly raised the pistol and stretched out his arm so that the weapon almost touched her forehead.

"Now," said Athos. "Give me the death warrant."

"I won't!" she cried.

"You have five seconds to hand it over," Athos said calmly, "or I shall use this pistol."

"Take it!" she finally screamed in a fury, pulling a single sheet of paper from a pocket in her dress, and throwing it at him.

Without lowering the pistol, Athos read the words that the Cardinal had written.

It is by my order and for the good of the state of

France that the bearer of this note is authorized to do what has to be done.

Signed: Richelieu

Athos quickly realized that the Cardinal had written a very clever death warrant without naming anyone. He could always deny later on that he had given her permission for the murders.

Athos put the paper safely away in his pocket. "Now, Madame," he said, "if you're mad enough to murder anyone else, you will have to do it in your own name. I intend to see you hang one day, but all in my own good time. I want you to live a little longer to give you plenty of time to think of that rope tightening around your neck."

With those last words, he left the room as quickly as he had entered it.

Before leaving the Red Dovecot Inn, he instructed his manservant, Grimaud, to take some local men and have Milady escorted to the nearest port, and put on a boat for England.

***

When Athos returned to his friends in the trenches, he was once more the quiet musketeer. All his anger had been used up on Milady.

D'Artagnan, Porthos, and Aramis were keen to hear what Athos had been up to.

"I will tell all," he said, "but the walls seem to have ears around here, as Milady discovered last night. No, before we discuss anything, let's find a place where we can't be overheard."

"Where better than the front line!" laughed Porthos. "Grimaud can make us a fine breakfast and we can talk in peace."

"What about the English?" inquired Aramis. "Isn't it just possible they'll try and kill us, so close to the front?"

"Well, we can be killed here as well as there," said Athos. "And we will have the benefit of dying with a full stomach. My man Grimaud is an excellent cook."

"It's settled then," said Porthos. "We can defend ourselves between glasses of wine and fine food. Let's go!"

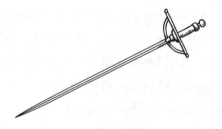

Chapter 19

Plotting and Planning

The four friends set off for the front line, along with Athos' manservant Grimaud, who was carrying a basket of food. The place they chose for their picnic was just a few hundred yards from the main town gate.

The English watched in amazement as the five mad Frenchmen set up camp right under their noses. The trench was just deep enough to keep their heads safe from the English gunners on the battlements of La Rochelle.

Athos, who was in a humorous mood, took off his hat, put it on the end of his sword, and waved it in the air. He just wanted to taunt the English gunners on the battlements of La Rochelle.

The English fired a dozen volleys, ripping his hat to pieces.

The trench held the bodies of several Englishmen who had been killed earlier skirmish.

"Don't worry," said Aramis, seeing Athos rather upset at the sight. "They can't hear us. And now, Grimaud, prepare the breakfast."

The four men sat down cross-legged, opened a couple of bottles of wine, and filled their glasses. They raised a cheer each time an English musket ball fizzed over their heads.

They were about to start talking when Athos saw some English soldiers edging towards them down one of the trenches. "Excuse me a moment," he said. "I think we have some visitors."

Grimaud was closest to the English and announced that twenty soldiers were about a hundred yards off.

"Good," said Athos. "We still have time to finish our wine."

With glasses emptied, the four men lined up their muskets and fired. Five Englishmen died, and fifteen retreated.

"There really is nothing more disagreeable than being disturbed at breakfast," complained Aramis, before instructing Grimaud to reload the muskets and bring on the bread and cheese.

The musketeers returned to their breakfast.

"Now," said D'Artagnan, "where is Milady—or Anne de Brueil as we know her now?"

Athos removed a sheet of paper from his pocket. "I took the opportunity last night to persuade my former wife to give me the Cardinal's death warrant. I now give it to you, D'Artagnan, for safekeeping. But the fact she has no death warrant doesn't mean she won't carry out the death sentences. I have sent her back to England, but we must be on our guard all the time."

"That woman needs her neck twisted," said Porthos. "She may be on her way to England but she still worries me."

"She worried me in England and in France," said Athos.

"She worries me everywhere," said D'Artagnan.

"She is out of our way for the moment," said Athos, "but she is probably already writing to the Cardinal, asking for a new warrant."

Grimaud gave a warning of more English troops on the way. "There are many more this time," he said.

Aramis suggested it was time to leave.

"Impossible," said Athos. "Firstly, we haven't finished breakfast. Secondly, we haven't finished our discussion."

Four muskets blasted out. Four Englishmen died. Forty-six others took off back to safety.

"Now, where were we?" said Porthos, once more handing the muskets to Grimaud to reload.

D'Artagnan suggested that perhaps he should go to England again, and find and kill Milady before she had a chance to murder anyone.

Athos interrupted. "Why should we try to save the lives of two Englishmen? After all, we are at war with England."

"The Duke and the Queen love each other," said D'Artagnan. "And I feel obliged to help Lord de Winter. I gave him mercy the last time we met."

It was finally agreed that Planchet should return to England with letters warning the Duke and Lord de Winter of Milady's death threats.

Once more, the discussion was interrupted by another warning from Grimaud; this time a whole regiment of English soldiers were on their way. The musketeers finally decided it was time to go.

Grimaud had done some additional preparation for this latest invasion of their private meeting. He had dragged several of the bodies of the dead Englishmen and placed them in a lying-down position on the edge of the trench with their guns pointing toward the English.

A great battle followed as the English killed their dead several more times before returning to their own lines. Grimaud and the musketeers laughed all the way back to camp.

Chapter 20

Arrested!

Planchet safely completed his journey to England with the warnings for the Duke of Buckingham and Lord de Winter. He brought back a short note from the Duke.

Thank you, gentlemen, for your warning. You may rest assured that all that needs to be done will be done.

Planchet's return to France had coincided with Milady's arrival back in England. Despite having given Athos the Cardinal's death warrant that was now in D'Artagnon's possession, she was more determined than ever to kill the Duke and Lord de Winter.

She checked into an inn close to her intended victims. It was just a mile from Lord Buckingham's country estate, and a stone's throw from Lord de Winter's home.

Disguising herself as an old woman, the assassin spied out the lay of the land for several days. She befriended several of the servants who worked at the two lords' houses, learning when their masters came and went. No one suspected a sweet old woman of plotting murder . . .

Milady decided to visit Lord Buckingham's house first, little realizing that her intentions were known. From the moment the Duke had received his warning, he had put his guards on alert.

She finally arrived at her target in the dead of night and crept up to the Duke's bedroom. She paused for a moment, outside the door. All was

quiet, except for the sound of faint snoring. Slowly, she crept into the room.

The moonlight caught the moment as she lifted high her long-bladed dagger.

With a maniacal shriek of hatred, she plunged the knife into the figure she saw lying beneath the bedclothes.

That was the moment when the Duke and Lord de Winter stepped out of the shadows, their swords pointing at the lady's heart.

At first, Milady had stared about her wildly, not understanding what was happening. "But you're dead!" she shouted at the Duke. "I've just killed you!"

"You killed a dummy, madam," replied the Duke.

Milady tried to think who could have warned the Duke and Lord de Winter. She knew she must have been overheard while talking to the Cardinal in the Red Dovecot Inn. She cursed her misfortune. It must have been D'Artagnan and his three friends!

Milady was escorted to Dover Castle, where she was locked away in a small cell in a tower, all by herself. And there she plotted during every waking moment how to take her revenge on the man who she knew had put her there— D'Artagnan!

Chapter 21

Milady's Devilish Charms

In the castle tower, Lord de Winter put Milady under the special guard of Captain John Fenton, a sea captain whose ship lay just offshore.

As the days passed, a most surprising change came over Milady. The violent scowl and constant look of hatred vanished from her face. She even smiled when Captain Fenton brought her food, and began long amusing conversations with him.

The captain became enchanted with his

prisoner. He found it hard to imagine she was an assassin. Indeed, she spent many hours explaining to the captain how she never had been one. Why, she knew she was stabbing a dummy on the night of her arrest. She had been told that it was just an exercise planned by the Duke to see if his guards stayed awake at night.

"But the moment I stabbed the dummy," said Milady so innocently, "they arrested me. It had something to do with my brother-in-law, Lord de Winter. He always wanted me dead so he could inherit my fortune. The Duke and Lord de Winter are close friends, so no doubt they are in this together."

Then she burst into tears and collapsed into the captain's arms.

Just then, footsteps were heard outside. Milady quickly disentangled herself from the captain and sat down on her hard prison bed.

The door opened to reveal Lord de Winter. "Captain," he said, "I want to remind you how dangerous this woman is. You must not enter her cell again. Use the flap in the door to leave her food in the future.

"This lady may look as beautiful and innocent as a child. But she is guilty of more crimes than you and I could fit in during a whole lifetime. She is young and beautiful, but still a monster. She uses her beauty to entrap victims like a spider. Be warned!"

Lord de Winter then pointed at her left shoulder. "She bears the brand of the Fleur-de-Lis; the mark of the hangman. That mark tells her life story."

At the mention of the word *hangman*, Milady dramatically slumped back on to her bed as if unconscious. In truth, she could still see her captors. She possessed that great art studied by so many women; the ability to look through her long eyelashes without appearing to open her eyes.

Captain Fenton was blind. All he saw was a beautiful young woman in need of help.

Over the next six days, Milady worked hard to charm Captain Fenton. On the first day, she swore an oath to him that there was no Fleur-de-Lis branded on her shoulder. "I would show you," she said, "but modesty prevents me from revealing my shoulder to a stranger."

The next day she covered her face with white powder. The captain was sure she was dying. She called for a doctor, and then told Captain Fenton to cancel her request. She would rather die, she said.

On the third day, she discovered religion and spent the whole day in prayer.

On the fourth, Captain Fenton found that she had unraveled the wool from her cloak and made a rope to hang herself from the beam of her cell. "Let me kill myself," she begged dramatically. "My life is one long torture. How can this world be so unkind to me?"

The captain took the rope away, saying she must wait. "We will prove your innocence," he said.

That same day, Lord de Winter informed Milady that she would be sent to London in two days' time. "You shall have a fair trial," he said, "but there will be only one outcome . . . the Duke of Buckingham will sign your death warrant and the

hangman shall end your life!"

"Blessed death!" she cried, with one eye on Captain Fenton. "How I will welcome it. God in Heaven knows I am innocent. The good Lord will welcome me."

On the fifth day, she snatched Fenton's knife and stuck it in her side; although carefully making sure only to scratch herself. "There, you see," she cried, as she fell to the floor, blood pouring from her side, "only an innocent woman would stab herself."

Lord de Winter was called. "Be calm, Fenton," he said. "She will not die of the wound. Witches don't die so easily."

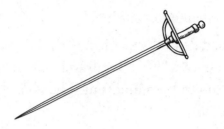

Chapter 22

Escape!

In spite of Lord de Winter's advice, the lovelorn Captain Fenton soon convinced himself that Milady was a victim of some plot between Lord de Winter and the Duke of Buckingham. He decided he would help her escape.

"I cannot bear it any longer," he whispered to his beloved, "to see an innocent so tortured."

"I knew you would save me!" Milady cried, like a helpless woman.

On the night of the sixth day, Milady was pacing her cell like a caged lion when she heard a tapping sound at the barred window. It was Fenton. He had scaled the castle wall with a rope ladder. He produced a large file and started to work away at the main window bar.

The first light of dawn was just visible on the horizon when at last Fenton cut through the bar. He pulled Milady through the window and together, they climbed down into the deserted main street of Dover Town.

"This way, Milady!" whispered Fenton. "I have my ship and crew ready to pick us up on the beach."

"Wait, my dear man," she said. "How can I leave without avenging myself on the Duke of Buckingham? How much do you love me, dear Captain Fenton? Enough to kill the Duke?"

"Enough to go to the ends of the earth for you!" he replied, going down on one knee and kissing her hand. "Besides, the Duke deserves to die. He has cruelly mistreated you. Wait by the boat. This shouldn't take long."

Milady gave him one of those tempting looks that would have enslaved a king. That look was enough to turn Fenton into her personal executioner.

He rushed off, found himself a horse, and galloped away. A half-hour's ride found him outside the Duke's country estate. The house had been completely unguarded since Milady's arrest. So Fenton, sword in hand, quickly found his way inside and up to the Duke's bedroom.

The sleeping Duke never woke again.

Fenton galloped back to Dover, only to find that there was no sign of Milady. She had disappeared. Then he looked out to sea. The sun was just creeping up over the horizon. Fenton saw his ship in the distance. Now under full sail, the ship had already set a course for France.

The captain fell to his knees and howled. He knew he had been fooled by the best actress in England.

Looking down on that scene with a spy-glass was Lord de Winter, who had just discovered Milady's empty cell. He saw Fenton's ship sailing for France and he could just see Milady, walking on the main deck.

The sight of Fenton alone on the beach told Lord de Winter all he needed to know. He hurried down to the beach with some of his guards. They found Fenton still lying on the ground weeping.

"The woman tricked me," he sobbed. "She said she would wait for me. Now she's stolen my ship."

Fenton made an immediate confession of what he had done that morning. "I've done a dreadful thing," he wept. "I've killed the Duke of Buckingham!"

Poor Fenton was taken away and locked in a castle dungeon.

***

When Milady arrived back in Calais, the last thing she wanted was for the musketeers to find out that she had returned. So, rather than travel on to Paris, she sent a messenger to the Cardinal, asking him and Rochefort to meet her.

A few hours later the messenger returned. The

Cardinal and Rochefort would meet her by the Gallows' Crossroads just outside Lille, midway between Calais and Paris. That location was a little too familiar to Milady. It was a place of terrifying memories for her . . . and it was about to give her one last nightmare.

Unfortunately for Milady, the messenger she had chosen to deliver her message to the Cardinal was a friend of D'Artagnan's man, Planchet. So news of the plan quickly reached the musketeers' ears.

By the time the Cardinal and Rochefort set off for Lille, D'Artagnan, Athos, Porthos, and Aramis had already raced there and hidden themselves in the trees above the crossroads. They were in a perfect position to hear what was said below.

Milady arrived soon after, followed by the Cardinal and Rochefort.

"The Duke of Buckingham is dead," said Milady, nervously looking up at the gallows looming above the crossroads. "And there is no blood on my hands. I persuaded a lovelorn Englishman to do the job for me."

The Cardinal looked very severe. "A few days ago, your news would have made me happy," he said, "but I have just heard that we have thrown the English out of Rochelle. Their army has returned to England. The war is over. King Charles is ready to sign a peace treaty with King Louis."

"But why should that change things?" asked Milady, looking a little concerned.

"To be truthful," said the Cardinal, "I think it would be unwise of me to be involved in the murder of an English Duke—particularly King Charles' War Minister. King Louis might thank me in private for killing his queen's lover. But in public, he would deeply regret such an awful murder now that peace has come and he has to be friends with King Charles."

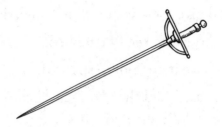

Chapter 23

Milady Alone

A dreadful look of fear crossed Milady's face as she realized that she was now on her own. The Cardinal was throwing her to the wolves to protect himself.

"But you signed a warrant for his death!" she protested.

"Did I?" said the wily old Cardinal, who had already learned through his spies that Athos had stolen it. "I can't remember."

"You did give me a warrant!" Milady cried.

"Then show it to me," he replied.

"I don't have it anymore," she said.

"In that case," said the Cardinal, "I can't be sure it ever existed. What say you, Rochefort?"

"Oh indeed, sir," was the reply. Rochefort knew better than most that it was always advisable to stay on the Cardinal's side.

High up in a tree, Athos heard the Cardinal's words and realized that Milady was on her own. Her powerful friends were ready to betray her. He whispered to D'Artagnan that he had something to do. "Whatever happens, wait for me here," he said. "I won't be long."

Athos slithered down the tree and ran off toward the town center of Lille.

Meanwhile, Milady was fighting for her life. "My Lord Cardinal," she begged, "I have served you well for many years. I have killed many of your enemies and risked life and limb for you."

"And it has been much appreciated," replied the Cardinal. "But you have put me in an unfortunate position by murdering, or being responsible for the murder of, one too many people. Namely, the Duke of Buckingham. But I will grant you your life. You have disappeared before. You can do it again."

Milady saw her escape, but asked the Cardinal one last favor. "Would you object if I kill one more of your enemies? He is to blame for my downfall."

"I presume you mean the musketeer, D'Artagnan," said the Cardinal. "He is of no matter to me. Do with him what you will."

With that, the Cardinal and Richelieu walked over to where they had tethered their horses. It was a strange thing, but instead of two horses, there were now three. The third horse was grazing quietly by the other two when the Cardinal and Rochefort approached.

"It's a runaway horse," said Rochefort, "and a mangy old creature at that. I think I've seen it somewhere before."

Rochefort was about to climb onto his own horse when the mystery animal suddenly reared up with its legs flying and then turned and kicked the count high into the air. Rochefort didn't hear the muffled chuckles from D'Artagnan, hiding above him in a tree.

Methuselah had finally taken his revenge on Rochefort, the man who one day long ago dared to insult the noble old horse.

"I told him not to insult my horse!" D'Artagnan whispered to his friends, holding back a laugh.

After the Cardinal and Rochefort had ridden off, Milady remained motionless. She realized that for the first time in her life she was alone. There was no one to help her now. It was almost dark. Not a sound was to be heard. A ghostly breeze moved silently through the tree tops. The nearby gallows rope swung to and fro.

Suddenly Milady turned her head. She had heard something. A flickering light was coming through the trees.

"Mon dieu!" she murmured, under her breath. "What's this?"

A figure, covered from head to foot in a

red, hooded cloak and carrying a lamp, slowly walked into the center of the crossroads.

Milady didn't move. She was frozen to the spot. "Who are you?" she said, trying to hide her desperate fear. "What are you doing here?"

"We have met before, Madame," answered the figure in a slow, echoing voice. "Surely you remember me."

"Who are you?" cried Milady a second time, sounding very frightened indeed. "Show yourself! Remove your hood."

The figure moved towards Milady. "Perhaps you will recognize me if I come a little closer."

The figure had almost reached Milady when the man inside the red cloak removed the hood and raised his lamp . . .

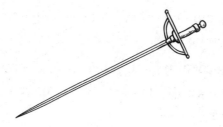

Chapter 24

The Hangman of Lille

Milady's scream was followed by a shriek and a screech, as she collapsed to the ground in shock.

"So you do recognize me after all," said the man. "I said farewell to you once and never expected to see you again."

At that moment, Athos appeared from the edge of the wood and walked up to Milady, who was now shaking uncontrollably. "We both know who this man is, don't we, Milady," he said, enjoying a moment of supreme revenge. "Go on, tell me who he is!"

Milady tried to control her shaking body and finally managed to speak. "The Hangman of Lille," she stuttered.

"Yes, Milady," said Athos. "You remember him well, don't you? Was it not on these very gallows that he hanged you?"

"No! No! No!" she screamed in terror. "Send him away!"

"Wasn't he the one who branded you with the Fleur-de-Lis, Madame?"

Even then Milady tried to deny it. "You have the wrong person," she insisted.

D'Artagnan, Porthos, and Aramis appeared, as the hangman took a step forward and tore the dress from Milady's left shoulder. She screamed again as the lamp cast shadows on the symbol of the Fleur-de-Lis.

"Your crimes are many," said the hangman. "You killed Athos' parents, your husband, and many others. Your time has come."

"Yes, it is time," said Athos grimly.

"I am rich," she pleaded. "I will give you a fortune if you let me go."

"Prepare yourself!" ordered Athos.

"Surely you would not hang a woman," begged Milady. "A musketeer would never hang a woman."

"You are not a woman," said Athos. "You are a demon escaped from hell. And that is where we are sending you back to."

Athos took hold of the struggling woman and began dragging her to the gallows.

"Pray God forgive me," she wailed. "I will become a nun and spend the rest of my life praying for my forgiveness. Let me live!"

It was too late. Athos had now pulled her up the steps to the gallows. The rope was placed around her neck.

Athos had a final question for Milady. "Perhaps you will tell us where you have hidden Mademoiselle Bonacieux. My friend D'Artagnan would be most happy to hear your answer. He might be even more generous than me and let you live, if the answer is a good one."

Milady knew it was her last chance and blurted out her answer. "She is in the Bastille under a false name."

"What name?" asked Athos.

"Dubrow," answered Milady.

She was about to say something else. But Athos had heard all he wanted to. He signaled to the hangman.

Milady would not return to haunt Athos again.

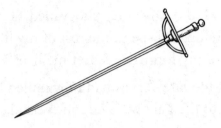

Chapter 25

In the Bastille

D'Artagnan, Athos, Porthos, Aramis, and their menservants returned to Paris. On the way back, they planned how to free Mademoiselle Bonacieux from the Bastille, the most secure prison in France.

It was D'Artagnan who came up with an idea. The Bastille had a new governor. The job was his reward for helping the Cardinal. That man was Monsieur Bonacieux, the greedy uncle of Mademoiselle Bonacieux.

D'Artagnan, who knew it was he who had spied on Mademoiselle Bonacieux during the matter of the Queen's diamond brooch, was eager to take revenge on the two-faced Bonacieux.

That night, the four musketeers arrived at the Bastille and told the guards on the main gate that they wanted to see the governor. "Tell him we're here on the Cardinal's business!" said Porthos.

A few moments later, the four men were led into Bonacieux's office.

"It's always nice to see someone on the Cardinal's business," said the unsuspecting Bonacieux. "What can I do for you?"

All four musketeers whipped out their swords, swishing them through the air just an inch or two from Monsieur Bonacieux's nose.

"What's this?" gasped the man. "I shall call the guards!"

"You won't call the guards," said D'Artagnan. "You'll lead us straight to Madame Dubrow's cell."

"Madame Dubrow?" asked Bonacieux. "I know nobody of that name."

"Yes you do, you miserable wretch," shouted D'Artagnan. "We're talking about Madame Dubrow whom the world, and you especially, know as Mademoiselle Bonacieux. Your niece!"

Bonacieux froze. "There must be some mistake. I would not allow my niece to be thrown into a dungeon."

"You lie!" roared D'Artagnan. "Take us to her now!"

With four swords at his back, Bonacieux led them through a maze of corridors and down several stone staircases.

Down and down they went, the air becoming fouler the deeper they went. All the way down the musketeers heard the groans and cries of prisoners who had not seen daylight for years. The only light came from the occasional candle hanging on the dripping wet stone walls.

At last they reached a great vaulted chamber that had been carved out of solid rock beneath the Bastille. A dozen cells led off it.

Bonacieux pointed to one. "Mademoiselle

Bonacieux is in there," he said.

"The key, please," said D'Artagnan.

The door was opened and a faint voice was heard coming from the cell. "Who's there?"

"Me!" replied D'Artagnan. The young man took a candle that was hanging on the outside of the door and went in.

Mademoiselle Bonacieux, as white as a sheet and blinking at the light, was lying on a dirty bed of straw. "D'Artagnan," she said weakly. "Is it really you?"

There was no time for talking now. The musketeers wanted to get out of the Bastille as soon as possible.

Mademoiselle Bonacieux was too weak from starvation, damp, and cold to walk up the long staircases. So D'Artagnan picked her up and laid her across his broad young shoulders.

"Now monsieur," said D'Artagnan, pricking Bonacieux with his sword, "perhaps you would like to try this cell for yourself."

Bonacieux went down on his knees, begging

not to be put in the dungeon.

None of the musketeers had any sympathy for the man. They lifted him up and threw him inside, locking the door behind him.

The four musketeers ignored the pitiful cries of Bonacieux from below, and hurried up the series of staircases. They had expected some opposition from the Bastille guards, but the sight of four musketeers in full flight sent them scurrying for cover.

At last they reached ground level and the corridor that led to the main gate.

It was only then that they saw real trouble ahead. Between them and the main gate stood four familiar faces, Cardinal's men all . . . Jussac, Bernajoux, Bicarat, and Cahusac.

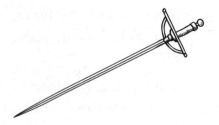

Chapter 26

The Final Battle

"We meet again, gentlemen," said Jussac. "You'll be pleased to know that I have a warrant for your arrest, signed by the Cardinal. The charge is murder of a state servant, one Milady, otherwise known as Anne de Brueil."

D'Artagnan gently lowered Mademoiselle Bonacieux to the ground.

"She can go," said Jussac. "We have no fight with Mademoiselle Bonacieux."

"Go to my apartment and wait for us," said D'Artagnan. "We won't be long in dealing with these ankle-biters."

Mademoiselle Bonacieux nodded and limped slowly away, blinking at the lamplight in windows she passed, as she'd been kept in the dark for so long.

"Right," said D'Artagnan to his fellow musketeers. "What do we do? Shall we give ourselves up to the Cardinal? Or shall we take on his bullies?"

"There's only one answer to that," said Porthos.

"Indeed," said Athos.

"All for one," roared Aramis.

"One for all!" cried D'Artagnan.

The four companions drew their swords and advanced.

Never had there been such a battle between the King's Musketeers and the Cardinal's Guards. D'Artagnan found himself fighting Jussac again. Athos played with Bernajoux, while Porthos and Athos attacked Bicarat and Cahusac.

But this time, there was no victor. The eight men, bloodied and boasting a score of cuts and other wounds, fought each other to a standstill.

It was D'Artagnan who finally called for the fight to end. "The honors are even," he said. "If we fight any longer we'll all be cut to pieces and be no good to either King or Cardinal. I'm not worried about facing the Cardinal. I'll answer his charge of murder. And answer it well."

The others were not so sure. "You're mad," said Porthos.

"I give you my solemn word," said D'Artagnan. "None of us will come to any harm by facing the Cardinal. My life on it!"

Reluctantly, the other musketeers agreed. An hour later, they entered the Cardinal's chamber. He stared in amazement at the bloodied state of both the four musketeers and his guards.

"I thought the war was over," he said.

Porthos answered for the musketeers. "The war between Musketeer and Guard will never end, sir," he roared.

"I beg to differ," said the Cardinal. "You stand charged with murder and it's very likely that after the evidence is heard, and a good hanging completed, there will be no four musketeers to fight any more. Do you deny hanging Milady?"

Athos, Porthos, and Aramis looked to D'Artagnan, as if expecting him to answer for them all.

"My Lord Cardinal," said D'Artagnan. "We do not deny it."

"Then there is nothing else to say," replied the Cardinal. "You admit your guilt."

"No, my lord," said D'Artagnan. "We admit to hanging her but not to our being guilty of it. Another man is guilty of the charge you make against us."

"And who might that be?" asked the Cardinal, becoming rather irritated with D'Artagnan's wordplay.

"You, my lord!" said D'Artagnan.

The Cardinal was astonished. "Be careful, young man," he said. "Just be glad that you will be hanged and have a quick death. Jest with me again and you'll not be so lucky."

"I do not jest," insisted D'Artagnan. "I have the evidence that you are the one guilty of allowing Milady to be murdered."

"You have a minute to explain yourself," hissed the Cardinal.

D'Artagnan slowly pulled a sheet of paper from his pocket. The Cardinal went quite white. He knew exactly what was written on that paper because he himself had signed it. But he had never expected to see that paper in D'Artagnan's hand.

D'Artagnan read it out.

It is by my order and for the good of the state of France that the bearer of this note is authorized to do what has to be done.

Signed: Richelieu

It was Cardinal de Richelieu's carefully worded authorization for Milady to kill the musketeers, the Duke of Buckingham, and Lord de Winter. It was the very same warrant that Athos had taken from Milady in the Red Dovecot Inn and given to D'Artagnan.

The Cardinal was silent for a full minute while he thought about the warrant.

D'Artagnan interrupted his thoughts.

"I think I can safely say that the warrant gave us the right to kill her for the good of France, and to kill her in your name. It's either that, or you having to admit that you authorized Milady to kill not just us, but the Duke of Buckingham, the King of England's most important minister. And I don't think King Charles would take too kindly to that. It could mean war between our two countries again."

The Cardinal knew he was beaten. "Well, gentlemen," he said, his voice suddenly becoming much quieter and gentler. "I don't think we have much more to do here today. You are free to leave."

The Cardinal was not too disappointed that he could not have the musketeers hanged. The truth of the matter was that he had actually been relieved to hear of Milady's death. Her murderous activities had even begun to frighten him a little, and he knew he could never completely trust her. Even though he had suggested Milady disappear at their last meeting, he hadn't believed that she truly would.

He would solve the problem of D'Artagnan and his three friends another day . . .

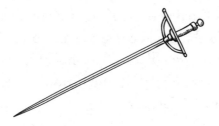

Chapter 27

Wedding Bells

The next mission for Athos, Porthos, and Aramis was an unusually peaceful one—escorting D'Artagnan on the day he married Mademoiselle Bonacieux. It was an unusual day, because the four musketeers were not involved in a single fight.

The guest list included the Queen, who was still broken-hearted over the murder of the Duke of Buckingham. But she took great comfort from D'Artagnan marrying her favorite lady-in-waiting.

The Cardinal and the King were both there too. The Cardinal had come to admire D'Artagnan a great deal. Even though it was the young man's wedding day, the Cardinal asked him again to join his Guards.

But D'Artagnan would never leave the King's Musketeers.

***

So the years passed. D'Artagnan eventually became the commanding officer of the King's Musketeers when Captain Treville retired.

Athos stayed with him for several years, but eventually fulfilled his ambition to be a priest.

Porthos and Aramis retired and bought the Red Dovecot Inn. In later years, they would pull up comfortable chairs by the fire and remember old times ... occasionally, rather mischievously, listening to private conversations from the room above where Milady had once stayed.

For Monsieur Bonacieux, the shock of being locked in a dungeon was too much. He ended his spying days and joined the church.

The Count de Rochefort never forgave D'Artagnan for making such a fool of him but he had learned a lesson . . . he would never insult old horses again.

Those brave musketeers—all for one, one for all—had made sure of that!

The End

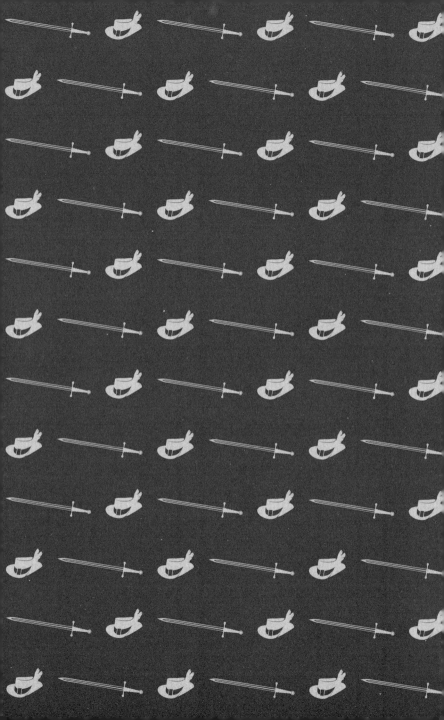